BLOOD SPLATTERED ON THE PAPER

By Violet Monday

Copyright © 2006 by MICHELLE H. RYDBERG

All rights reserved.

No part of this book may be reproduced without written permission from the publisher or copyright holders, except for a reviewer who may quote brief passages in a review; nor may any part of this book be reproduced, stored in a retrieval system, or transmitted in any form or by any means electronic, mechanical, photocopying, recording or other, without written permission from the publisher or copyright holders.

Also Available at:
City Lights Bookstore - www.citylights.com
The Beat Museum - www.thebeatmuseum.org
Anno Domini // www.galleryAD.org
Phoenix Books - www.dogearedbooks.com/phoenix

Contact Mail:
P.O. Box 2032
Santa Clara, CA
95055

Contact:
Violet_Monday@yahoo.com

Cover by Josh Gillick of Artist Films
Edited by David Winterstein
ISBN 978-0-6151-5506-7
Library of Congress Catalog Control Number: 0-615

Manufactured, typeset and printed in the United States of America

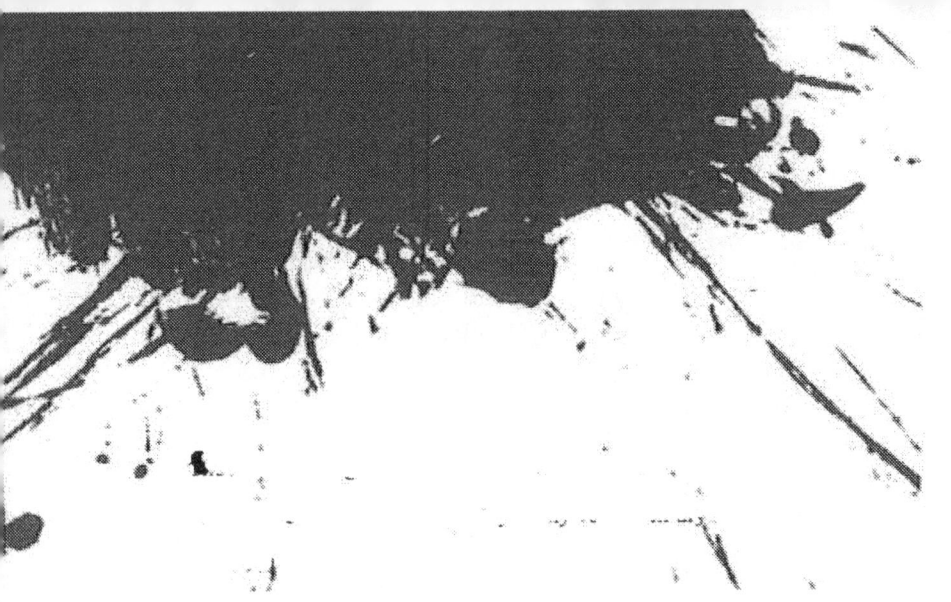

Dedication

To my Family, Ed, Nancy, Fred, Edna
Special Thanks to Catherine

Table of Contents

In the Beginning 11

KA 13
    CELLBLOCK #9 14
    BITCHES 16
    MOTHER NATURE!?! 17
    8th WEEK 18
    ALONE 20
    SOME PARTNER IN CRIME 21
    MELTING 22
    HE IS LIFE'S PUNCH LINE 23
    ANCIENT ONES 24
    A FRAGILE HEART 26
    SONIC BOOM 27
    THE DIRECTOR 28
    CHAOS 29
    BLEEDING IN PUBLIC 30
    SKELETON 31
    TWIST IT 32
    NEW OBSESSION 33
    LAND OF THE LIVING 34
    BOXED IN 35
    ONE NIGHT 36
    THE COAGULATED MOON 37

Love Rises From The Ashes 39
    DOUBLE ENTENDRE 41
    THE SOLUTION 42
    I LIKE HER BETTER 43
    POP ICONS 44
    FALLING ASLEEP IN CLASS 45
    HOLLYWOULD AND WINE 46
    CAR CRASH 47
    MISTRESS OF THE NIGHT 48
    MISTAKES DISSLOVED IN WATER 49

DREAMER	50
PITY PARTY	51

DURING HIS BLACKOUTS 53

O.D.	55
DESPERATE COUPLE	56
THE BALLAD OF LITTLE JOE	57
IN THE SPACE SUIT	58
CAR CRASH	59
SOMETHING'S THERE	60
HEART PALPITATING	61
IMAGE	62
EMOTIONAL SHOTGUN	64
IDEAS	65
SURVIVING THE NIGHT	66
MISSING	67
THE ORANGE	68
THE WORLD IS OUR CRADLE	69

RELAX 71

MY HOOD	73
HIDDEN SECRET	74
HIP HOP KIDS	75
LAST NIGHT	76
MONEY DOESN'T MATTER	77

Keep On Moving 79

PLANS CRUMBLE	81
THE DEATH OF THE CAT	82
CLEO AND ME	83
LET GO	84
NOT UNTIL THE SUN GOES DOWN	85
SIZZLE FIZZLE	86
SOLACE IN YOUR MIND	87
SHY GIRL	88
EVENING SONG	90
UNLOCK HOPE	91
THE PERFECT LIFE	92

    WHERE THE TRUTH LIES 93
    TONIGHT 94
    SERPENT 95
    FEEL THE DANGER 96
    VENGEANCE 98

The Sun Peaks Out **101**

    YOU ARE SO FABULOUS 103
    MY STARLET 104
    THE GUEST 105
    SHE'LL NEVER FIND 106
    LAST NIGHT 108
    TWEAK PLEASE 109
    A MILLION DIRECTIONS 110
    WHEN THE LIGHT TURNS OUT 111
    ONLY YOU 113
    COMMUNICATE 114
    GOSH DAMN 115
    THE MURDERESS 116
    HE'S HAD IT 118
    EMOTIONALLY SLUTTY 119
    MISTREATED LOVERS 120
    OBSESSED 121
    CREATURE OF RANDOMNESS 122

Racing Thoughts **125**

    INSPIRATION 143

In the Beginning

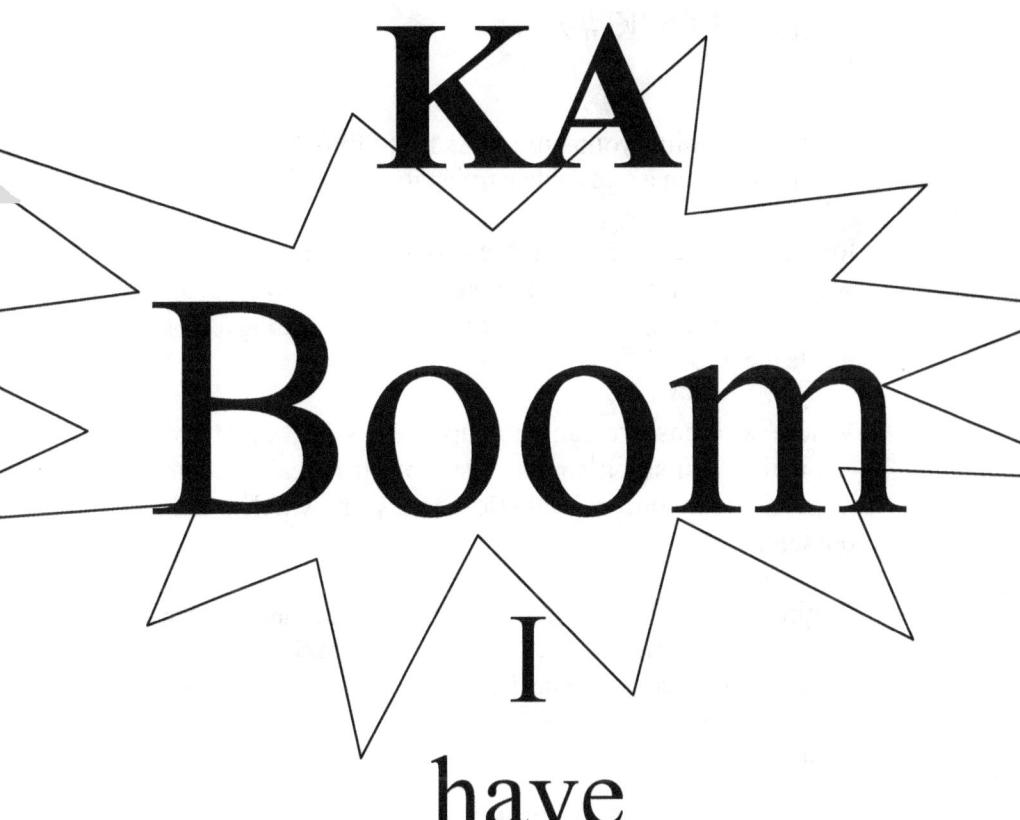

KA
Boom

I
have
an
idea
but
it
is
fading
away.
Damn
it

Staring outside at the beautiful day, behind the office desk the anxious business

CELLBLOCK #9

How is spending your time in 8x10 cellblock number nine different then the crime in a 6x8 cubicle trying to make a dime

looking through bars from the inside bare gray walls dreaming of the walk in a sun filled cherished park as the bored business man is looking down the halls fantasizing about getting out to get smashed inside the bars

Where wardens are sadistic supervisors go ballistic on your sore ass while You say it's pessimistic but it is realistic narcissistic and humanistic in our capitalistic society in which we have planted ourselves

Regimented hours to eat your meat three free meals for the incarcerated one unpaid office meal for one lousy hour come back early or skip your meal become rewarded for good behavior amongst your co-workers and friends as the inmate gets time shaved off of his sentence for good behavior

Where the guard locks and unlocks up the convict as the worker carries a security card and you unlock doors by yourself with security guards watching over you through a perverted surveillance camera looking at your face, name, tits, and ass, eyeing your stats through the computers database

woman is in deep thought about her direction in life as she is rubbing her aching

Sharing the same toilet with the last sloppy hole that sat down before you while the imprisoned gets their own toilet and trinkets All expenses paid trip to the big house by slaving taxpayers who want the streets clean of the filth the murderer left behind

It's the taxpayers that deduct from their precious pennies so the con artist can watch TV and play video games while the hard workers are paying for everything so who really is the one in solitary confinement

head which pulsates incessantly. "Oh great, I'm not going to meet the deadline," she

BITCHES

Did you know

Bitches,

Are not selective,
They are just

Bitches,

Who believe they are effective,

When it comes to friends,
I am selective,
Since I'm not a bitch,
I am protective

When those bitches start complaining,
I run for cover,
Because it starts raining.
And the ground,
It starts shaking,

Their claws scrape my chest
Yet my breast,
Protects my heart
And their words become a dart,
Thrown,
    At close range,
Those bitches!

looks at her computer clock. She is full of stress, tired, and with a headache. "This

MOTHER NATURE!?!

What happened to **Father Nature**?
Did he run off with the **Sister Sun**?

(Whose father was the **man in the moon**)

Leaving **Mother Nature**,

Our **Mother Earth** to fend
                         for herself
See what is happening without
                         his help

Little **April Showers** becomes
                       seduced by lightening
and thunder down under
            and vigilant eyes have no way
                     to pry as the dark cloudy night enshrouds them
                     from their protecting kin

Father Time
     left
                 Lady Luck
For **Madame Rain**

because

he
Thought SHE was a good f…f…f…

             Friend!!!

job is just not what I expected," she thinks in frustration as she feels a heavy darkness

8th WEEK

In the 8th week, he fished in his pant pocket for a pack of cigs
He then whispers the truth with his deep baritone trumpet sound
  to help guide you to the way
mysteriously
staring at you with his eyelids hung low
like a black cloak and two dark coals
heating towards you
with a smirk and a suck, inhale, and blow of a thin haze of
smoke
in your face

    As she hugged his ruff and rugged body, he slowly and languidly
    softened up
    like hot melted butter
    dripping to the floor
    through her fingers
    d
     r
     i
      p
       P
        I
         N
          G
           S
            L
             O
              W
             L
              Y

    shegrippedontohimfordearlife

come over her. The boss wants the paperwork done by noon, and it is a quarter till

but he left her grabbing empty air

only remnants of his soul floating upwards

as she looked up at the sky

noon and she is not done, and in fear of being fired at the end of the month because

ALONE

Alone
A lone

Al one

All one
One

The shallowness seeps into the new found friends

They return to the bedroom to form a group
A clique
Only to form a clique within the clique

Full of dry emotion that is propelled by the fulfillment of popularity,
Bubbly thoughts, produced smiles, exaggerated stories of boyfriends and their kisses, stimulating conversations about the gap, old navy, and banana republic,
How profound!?!
I am so lucky
I have found such a giddy group of friends

One
All one

Al one
A lone

Alone

the cuts are being made. The company is not making quota, and the budget is

SOME PARTNER IN CRIME

Some partner in Crime

In life
    f
      f
        f
          f
            f
              Lie

The lovers were stuck in a time zone of the unknown and one of its kind

he couldn't run away
Life
    f
      f
        f
          Lie
It kept following him
she could not stop it either

It kept overflowing
overwhelming
he just kept running
Leaving all of his cheating girlfriends
unwanted lovers, liars, flakes, fakes

Life
    f
      f
        f
          Lie

females with agendas, superficial friendships

slim. Day in and day out, she feels a calling of freedom. She thinks of her freedom

MELTING

The sun is boiling my blood underneath my skin

Please give me water or the valley of my veins will dry

Where is the ice?

Because my mouth is so dry,

Thank you, for leaving me here defenseless in the tightly sealed car

While the breeze moves outside,

And you spoon your boyfriend,

I cannot drink my own sweat beads because they are too salty and warm

My cry sounds like a drill cutting into a redwood tree,
My heart is begging me to move

 but

My legs are paralyzed and my arms are limp
My eyes are closing as my vision fades into darkness and solitude,

My breath becomes the earth
And the last sound I hear is my ears melting off.

in the world. What does she desire; her mind thinks about a beautiful forest where

HE IS LIFE'S PUNCH LINE

Why on that very night they unite
ignited tempestuous hearts
very first tryst
- Neither were in control
mixed soul
Why them – Why now?
No tomorrow's phone call
She's not home
She doesn't answer anymore –
whore,
It is going to be difficult to ignore
Her lore has rhythmical power
devour her beat
From head to feet that moved him so deep
weep, was it special for her?
Or just another Tuesday
just another lay, he asks himself not wanting to know the atrocious
truth
as his youth slips by the sunrise
A month passes, he sits on a barstool
near the divine pair
and stare, longing for her
no clue of her, curse that bittersweet night
her sight that lingers in his mind
All the time, bitter for his psyche, sweet for the heart
Why start then forever depart
curious about this devise
his demise
while holding another lightening rod
someone is laughing hysterically at him
across the ethereal divide,
a guide with red wine and eating the lamb

Because He is life's PUNCH LINE

she can lay at rest. The business woman sitting in her dull cubicle feels a sudden

ANCIENT ONES

Disaster is striking
the demon of madness and despair
is released from immemorial hiding places
Souls are harvested
and taken home to their place of origin
outside the solar system

That's when an ancestor came to me
and whispered through the wailing wind
in the starlight night
A sound like I've never heard before
like the opening of a door
a touch like I've never felt
and a scent I've never smelt

The ancient one came down upon
my breath and blew me a cold kiss
that shook me to the core
down to the ground
feeling shivers

When I was born I broke the chain to the ancestors
a battle is to arise
My parents were surprised

take hold of the night
gleaming with honeydew at our sight
walking through the grave
that our ancestor's have paved

breath in the chill of the fog
blow out it's demon

urge of madness surging throughout her robotic body. Her shoulders, neck, and

The air is thin
the fog is full
As dew surrounds me
As I stand in lush green grass
Admire the sparkling diamonds on each blade
reflecting my moonlight

As I await my challenge like the warrior of the night
ready for the battle I so long prepared for

back sharply tenses up just as her eyes are stiff and her brain sparks a fusion as she

A FRAGILE HEART

Tipping her with silent goodbyes
Mild grin and yellow eyes
That is his disguise

preying on young girls
Give them kisses and tell them lies

beating her in
And letting it out
Leave her hanging
Making sure to take a new route

Smelling fingers and combing hair

Where has he been

To the next affair

stops her computer typing, the cranking out of jumbled blurry numbers. The veins

SONIC BOOM

A Sonic Boom

A crash contorted
Screeching wheels
A hubcap flails
A fleshy thud onto the ground
A gasp for air
A cracked – splat - skull
From Ninety miles per hour
Velocity of the car
Mother could not have seen
The accident from so far

in her body want to explode as she wants to scream feeling insane with the monotonous

THE DIRECTOR

She is the director of her life

She takes the horn and blows it in the man's ear

"I'm not your wife"

Grab me a beer

she commands. And it is done.

Gently stroking her employer on the cheek and whispering,
"I will make this company grand and glorious,
let me work for you and you shall see."

Speeding away on a hotfoot to the tryst
vociferations bellows from her desperate friend
But it's too late…she's made her wend

To Paris and back!
She prowls around town with a cigarette sniffing out her prey,
spotting a sexy man, with champagne in his hand

She is waking up in Cannes and parting in Nice,
And back to Paris the next week.
It's her plan.

To keep up with her is
unfeasible
She eats her years
And spits them out in your face

work on that warm sunny day. The primal animal inside of her walks out of the office,

CHAOS

**MorningChaosNoonChaosNightChaosMorningChaos
NoonChaosNightChaosMorningChaosNoonChaosNight**

Blood splatters on the face of an innocent child,
It whips his face like shards of glass,
His nerves start to buzz,
Limbs vibrate like a temblor

**Morning Chaos Noon Chaos Night Chaos
MorningChaosNoonChaosNightChaos**

The young virgin,
Changed his whole facade,
Instead of playing football,
He lost his faith in God.

Morning Chaos Noon Chaos Night Chaos Morning Chaos

running to the porch, through the door, in the room, under the bed he felt God's tears touch his.

Morning Chaos Noon Chaos Night Chaos

His heart beats with fire,
Blazing at his breath

Morning Noon Night

and she confuses everyone around her with whispers, "Where is she going?"

BLEEDING IN PUBLIC

Are you willing to bleed for what you believe in
following a creed which could cost you your skin
an atrocious beating in the mass meeting
do not surrender to your contender
be the defender, do not settle for tender

a wave of blood blasts open the public door
exploding flash flood commences the war
are you willing to sacrifice your soul
will the beating take it's toll
are you willing to sacrifice your existence
find your persistence and evade resistance

"What's wrong with her?" "Hey, come back here, you have work to do!," a worried

SKELETON

breath in the life to the skeleton of verse
explore the lyrical bones to break the curse
unforeseen clues
bring to surface a broken bruise
mysterious cracks
perhaps from an axe
a verbal attack
creates the impact

a soul swirls and grooves,
floating, drifting, blowing, it moves

breathe in the heart to your poetic skeleton
close your eyes to recall your loved one
the rhymes flow in
penetrating the skin
a song beats out
without any doubt
rhythmic contractions
create inundated demonic actions
pumping bloody emotions through the veins
a soulful rap destroys the pains

stressed out man stands up from his desk as the woman leaves the corporate world

TWIST IT

I hope it twists your mind
makes it flip and burn
forget about time
just grab on
make your head turn
Relieve your mind
unwind with wine
forget the time

and never comes back. The woman is packing her suitcase at the goodbye party as

NEW OBSESSION

new obsession
leads to his only depression
it's you
Repression from his heart
suspension from the start

chasing you,
He'll never find
That path is dark
and does unwind

calling to you from the telephone
no one is ever home

her beloved friends and family surround her. "We are going to miss you," her best

LAND OF THE LIVING

He enters the land of the living

Where the blood drips in and out of the heart
The beat commences
The tempo trickles and squeals for more

The ride begins as he clutches for mother

holding her tightly

Where tangled Shadows grow and devour them gently

subconscious peaks out
Framing gestures
light begins
emotions start slow
grow
unfolding

friend throws confetti. "You're going to have a great time," her sister hugs

BOXED IN

> I hate to be so boxed in
> you judge due to the color of my skin
> my looks, my ass, my middle class
> With your arrogance
> Inheritance
> You make me wince
> You already have assumed

> Unfairly presumed
> I wouldn't like that film, dress ~ Music style
> You boxed me in, believing I'm not versatile,
> I'm not cool enough for you, miss holiness
> Almighty crowned princess, I guess

I hate to be so boxed in
You judge due to the color of my skin
my looks, my ass, my middle class
With your arrogance

> Almighty crowned princess, I guess
> After all your gossip
> And torment
> Death is the greatest equalizer
> Don't live in the present

Inheritance
You make me wince
You already have assumed
Unfairly presumed
I wouldn't like that film, dress ~ Music style
You boxed me in, believing I'm not versatile,
I'm not cool enough for you, miss holiness
Almighty crowned princess, I guess
After all your gossip
And torment

> I'm not
> cool
> enough for
> you, miss
> holiness
> Almighty
> crowned
> princess,
> I guess
> After all
> your
> gossip

> Death is the greatest equalizer
> Don't live in the present

"Take plenty of pictures for me, and don't forget to write," says her brother.

ONE NIGHT

She swallowed her pride
And other things
On that dark felt night
Driving to his home
As they lie there alone
In the stillness of the room

An erotic night
Then in the morning her flight

Even though
they hated each other
Just three months ago

Finding him annoying
then feeling some kind of urge
to purge
he called her to come over
she felt him up and over

"Sweetie, you do what you have to do. It sounds like the Peace Corp is your calling,

THE COAGULATED MOON

The coagulated moon hangs low
After the death outside of the child's home
He's 15 alone
During the black holiday
Sky shrieks as he fires
The first round
stars colliding
petrifying

Darkness stares at his
Pretty eyes
It's his disguise
Heart dropping into darkness
    LOWEr
           LOW er
                lower
he can only move forward
slicing reality in half
destroyed, unable to repair
past damaged and gone
regret, regret, not sure of regret
does he even feel this
after daily beating, slashes, ridicule
feeling miniscule, abuse
from his beloved father
bleak slaughter
staring at the threshold
in which he has commenced
touching the reality
feeling it's ripple effects
bouncing towards him
grim
with sin
from within

and you will be giving back to the earth…giving back to the world," her mother reaffirms. "Follow your passion, follow your heart and you will never be wrong" her

Love Rises From The Ashes

father is proud. "Bye my love, I will be waiting for you when you get back," her

DOUBLE ENTENDRE

It's the year of the cock and I woke up
early to sit next to the pussy willow drinking a
cocktail
under the warm afternoon sun stroking my pussycat as she lays their tired
and lazy like a
cockatoo

boyfriend quietly cries. The woman waves goodbye to her friends and family as she

THE SOLUTION

I desire the **ration** that can satisfy my passion
Give me the **prescription** to cure my addiction
I take the **pill** that cures the ill
Do you have the **drug** to fall in love
I want the **potion** that can alter my emotion
I need my **medicine** for my adrenaline
Order me a **whiskey sour** I'm feeling dour
Fetch me **vile** that makes me smile
Let us **smoke** for us to provoke
Take the **dose** so I can see the ghost
Fire up the **gases** to stop the masses
Where is the **liquor** that can remedy the bore
Insert the **shot** for your beauty spot
Take a **puff** to forget all that stuff
Where is the **vodka tonic** so I can feel bionic
I lack my **fix** to stop the ticks
Buy me the **brand** so I can expand
Bring in the **pump** so I can hump
Drink from the **bottle** to go full throttle
Get the **refill** to make me chill
Drink the **tea** to rehabilitate me
Finally the **supply** now say goodbye

gets on that plane to give back to the world where she finds the love inside. Love rises

I LIKE HER BETTER

She's never gotten high before
over forty, high strung and bored
on vacation she decides to paint the door
revamping the room and sweeping the floor

The fumes hit high
She begins to sigh
laughs hysterically
even gives me a hug

from the ashes.   *~The lonely woodsman receives a phone call from the police that*

POP ICONS

If a company sold a pop singer's poop,
people would buy it.
And if they told you it was good for you,
people would eat it

his estranged mother has died from a drug overdose, and they tell him where and

FALLING ASLEEP IN CLASS

Unable to move
FALlllliiiinnnngggg
into a deep trance

Eyelid's unnnnnnnn===lift----------able
nodding head in a bobbing dance
DOwn

       Down

              down

...oooO................
.....(....)...Oooo.......
.........(.....(....).......
.........._).....)../.........
................(_/..........

HEAD UP! STRAIGHT UP! With unkempt hair and droopy eyes
then
       Slowly
          Subtly
              DOWn
                  DOwn
                      Down
                            down
striving w/ no power
            being swallowed
                      very wallowed

by the man that slumbers

when the funeral is. "*Friday the 13th at 3 p.m.,*" *the policeman explains.* "*Yes, sir*

HOLLYWOULD AND WINE

Yeah it's so fine
so divine
Miss Hollywould with her wine
It's where she started her odd jobs she calls blow
she needed the dough
so she put on her fishnets
slicks back her hair
lipstick and hidden bulge
matching bra and underwear
It was her business
Miss Holly would for a dollar
you just need to holla
Just bring wine from the finest vine

thank you," the woodsman listens and takes in the news. They hang up, and the

CAR CRASH

Panic on the phone
you are on the other end
you crashed your car on the highway alone,
will he ever see you again,

Could this be it?
a tear trickles down your cheek,
crying and sighing and crying again
for he is mild weak and wild meek

For one last touch on his precious lips
its unfortunate but it was bound to happen

woodsman is stopped in his tracks and has to sit down. He ponders the situation and

MISTRESS OF THE NIGHT

We set up the scene
time and date
with nervous jitters
we await our fate

Create the scene
atmosphere
nervous jitters
what to wear

Create the costume
what to wear
motivation
atmosphere

create the fashion
create the scene
it's a mass production
beauty queen

Mistress of the heart
we keep finding ourselves
alone together
toget her
2get her
to
get
her
together

begins to cry. It is a feeling that he has not experienced in years. The stoic man is

MISTAKES DISSLOVED IN WATER

the conscious
&
unconscious
become blurred boundaries
be come

blur red
blu r red
blurred

Dissolving in water
Deep into the sea
The fish swim around her bloody floundering heart
As it dissolves in water
Uninhibited feelings
Slowly disappear
As the lake becomes clear
Dissipating fear
He plunges into the sea of feelings
No more need for anymore healings
Love becomes both
joy and sorrow
Into the world
of tomorrow

moved. The woodsman combs his beard and gets dressed in a dirty rustic brown suit

DREAMER

just a dreamer
if you say yes to his demands
Then you would be so happy
If not
It's only a dream
you can always
Al way s
All ways
Ways

find all ways to dream

different ways to go

always dreaming

always

To find another dream
There are other courses
find another dream
to ponder
How can one little person cause so much chaos?
"I didn't mean to cause trouble"
The little person might ask

It's just his dream

then drives from the forest to the city to attend his mother's funeral. He is nervous and

PITY PARTY

The Pity Party
Who will attend?

The dreamer with all of his dreams shot down
The self-motivator with all of his motivation gone
The thinker who says he is crazy
The self-believe who does not believe in himself
The planner who has no one to make plans with
The traveler with no one to travel with
The Sad story with no one to tell it to
The heavy heart with no one to share it with

anxious as he enters the funeral parlor. There is a small room full of his mother's friends and family members dressed in black just as he sees his sister crying and

DURING HIS BLACKOUTS

slowly approaching him. "Hi," his sister gives him a hug. He is touched by her

O.D.

We got high
We could fly
off the ground we saw sound
later on after our giggles
I noticed a reaction
that made me stare at him
he started to feel cold
then he was hot
his heart shot
bang, bang, bang
It wouldn't stop
Panic began...
Shock, shock, shock
The panic attack
is reaching the air
I'm very fearful
I really do care
I'm worried and carried
him to the hospital

warmth and he hugs her back. "How are you?," he slowly asks. "It's good to see

DESPERATE COUPLE

Two singles that wanted to become a pair
A couple that needed each other out of convenience

they just want to sleep their life away

Dream

And never come back

you. I haven't seen you in years," she pauses, "I've missed you." They both walk

THE BALLAD OF LITTLE JOE

Locked here in this closet,
This cold prison cell,
Tired of all the raging,
He feels like he's in hell.

What does…
Make his heart beat?
I'm afraid he lost his soul,
No love, No Passion,
He's uncertain of his goal.

He lost his mom and Grandma,
So, he only had himself,
Becoming an adult,
At an early age of twelve.

The only passion he ever felt
Was a need to leave the farm,
Too many horrible memories,
Left his heart with harm.

over to his mother's corpse and touch her beautiful skin and as he does this he feels a

IN THE SPACE SUIT

breathing

From the inside and out your mouth
Being controlled by something unknown

Your mind is being programmed by an alien and he is laughing as he made you trip on the stairs in front of your friends

Your leg shakes for no apparent reason and you find yourself at your crushes house

And you do not recall how you got there

are always looking to expand their horizon's.

sense of redemption washing over him. A blessing takes place as the mother, brother,

CAR CRASH

Panic on the phone
you are on the other end
you crashed your car on the highway alone,
will I ever see you again,

Could this be it?
a tear trickles down my cheek,
crying and sighing and crying again
for I am mild weak and wild and meek

For one last touch on his precious lips
its unfortunate but it was bound to happen

SOMETHING'S THERE

The soft energy hits the surroundings,
Footsteps following,
Vigilantly watches her eyes, actions,
Wants to kiss his lips
Care to dance and drink
Eat her cake.

Hiding in a cave for safety,
While the disparaging air surges and awaits it naive victim

HEART PALPITATING

Walking down the hard walkway
His body sweats
water drips out of his pores

he looks around and it feels like LOUD MUSIC IS SCREAMING
INTO HIS EARS
He's trying to act normal
BUT HE IS NOT
Everyone else is smiling
"Hello"
the passerby says
"How's it going?"

"Fine" he feigns

while inside he's panicked and frazzled
feeling like shards of glass
continuously fall and cut the inside of his chest

his nose flares
yet he tries to smile

young boy hears his parents fighting from the inside of his room as he tries to sleep at

IMAGE

At midnight Pamela's, home alone,
In the bathroom, she listens as the faucet drips,
scowling at what she sees in the mirror,
Black Lashes, brown eyes, a gray soul,
Regrets of the past and destruction of her future,
She cries in anger once again.

She contemplates her fate again,
Withdrawing from friends and family, alone,
With no hope for the future,
Listening as the tap water drips,
With her despondent soul,
A mess is what she sees in the mirror.

A hopeless singer is what she sees in that mirror,
She can't wake up with that face once again,
Slowly losing her soul,
She slowly loses energy, alone,
Quietly listening to the sound of drips,
Concentrating...because she can't find her future.

She yells in anger, "Fuck the future!"
A shattered mirror,
Then her blood drips,
She grabs the sharpest shard to deepen the cut again,
Falling to the ground alone,
She lost her soul.

On the ground Violet's lifeless soul,
Couldn't believe in a hopeful future,
A loser is what she saw in that mirror,
This is what she repeated to herself, again and again,
As the fluid, drip, drip, drips.

night. "You are drunk," his mother yells out. "What are you going to do about it?,"

Only the sound heard is the continuous drips,
A numb body with departure of the soul,
No will to begin again,
And to think about the future,
Shattered memories in this broken mirror,
As she lies alone.

Ended future,
A defeated soul,
For a girl who saw herself only alone.

his father fights back. The young boy puts the pillow over his head and tries to sleep

EMOTIONAL SHOTGUN

She carries an emotional shotgun
AK-47
Lock and load

Waiting for her next unsuspecting victim

Innocent or not
She is going to use it

It's already in her hand and under her coat

She can't wait until
she can pull the trigger, it's her release

In her mind she walks around
just waits until you say something rude

"go ahead and make fun of me, go ahead and fuck up," she says in her mind.

Dark shadowy eyes
What is going on in her mind?

as he hears the sound of a lamp being shattered to the ground through the wall.

IDEAS

Ideas crumble
like a broken statue
collapsing and rolling down to pure sedimentary rocks
watch it break

    Q
   OOooo
    Ooooo
     o o o o
    O O oo O ooo_____

   Shattering in your tearful eyes

with no one to help him
he cannot finish the sculpture alone
although he's tried
[no one cares]

looking for help
but no one is to be found
just the annoying sound of the lamp
buzzzzzzzzzzz*ing*buzzz*ing* buzz*ing

hating that sound
of emptiness
that's exactly what it sounds like

on the day he needs help
she is out of town
she is having special company over
she does not answer the phone
no one is home

shivers in tears. "Get out!," mother screams as her voice carries over, "get out!," her

SURVIVING THE NIGHT

Surviving the night
where chaos lays on top of you
given it to you straight up

Greed corrupts her heart as she uses you as her pawn in her
Queendom of vanity and destruction
her male workers adore her
yet the women want to destroy her

voice passes down the hallway and past his room, "get out!," to the front door. The

MISSING

We can only hope she's okay
we can only hope she's satisfied
Haven't heard from her in days

is she coming home
why doesn't she call on the phone
it's a mystery to me
where do you roam

young boy climbs out of his bed and moves the curtains from his window sill to see his

THE ORANGE

Cutting into the mid-morning orange
Slicing into two
Four
Slicing into 6
Slowly pulling the sharp knife up
Watching
The orange bleed juices from out of its insides
The thumb bleeds too
The orange and the thumb both bleed
Together in harmony

Devouring the wrinkly insides and licking the rim
The juices fall off the chin
Stinging the wound
But keep eating the orange

Cutting into the mid-morning orange
Slicing into two
Four
Slicing into 6
The orange juices increase as does the wound
The citrus thrusts out of its rind
Thumb and orange intertwine
In harmony

Sighing

Devouring the wrinkly insides and licking the rim, and the juices fall off the chin,
Stinging the wound, But kept eating damn the orange

mother pushing his father out of the house. The sound of harsh rumbling and

THE WORLD IS OUR CRADLE

We are all little babies and the world is our cradle
The grand order of design looks down upon us
& rocks us to sleep
Nuzzled all together under a fuzzy warm blanket

Like little fallen angels
With tiny little wings
Delicate to touch
Fragile with fear

Watching from heaven laughing
And itching his crotch
Watching the innocent sister inhale her last breath

Is it me or has the whole world gone mad

I'm not ready for the world and the world is not ready for me

Not good at being human
Not - @ - all

But we must remember that we are all little babies
And the world is our cradle

pushing is heard near the front door and she smacks him on the head, "goodbye," as the front door closes. Father runs and rustles through the leaves as he jumps in the

car to start the engine and quickly peels out and speeds away. A moment of silence

MY HOOD

Tonight was such a lovely night.
Even the crack dealers took a rest from their perches
The air was so fresh and clean running past my nose

What a bright light
Bursting through the shivering darkness

Our bodies blend and disappear
Breathless
Eager
Gleaming
In your arms
I am reborn
In the thick translucent night
We live forever in this instant

sweeps through the house as mother sighs and then slowly walks back to her bedroom.

HIDDEN SECRET

She is America's best hidden secret
like an angel
Invisible-hiding in the walls
At night, the fairy leaps in your dreams
tiptoeing like a ballerina encircling the ritual of love
She knows all- muhahaha
That you never did!

Waking up the next morning to an awkward silence, the young boy finds that only his

HIP HOP KIDS

Last night the street
was more beautiful
than I last remembered
TO BRAKE IT DOWN
THE HITS, THE CUTS, THE BEATS
    They were all bad asses
Kids spinning - mixing- beating- changing life up
pop'n- crawling, jamming with a twist of kicks
heads buzz'n - tweaken, creakin'
it was all beautiful
more beautiful than I last remembered

mother is in the kitchen, and she fakes a broken smile while nervously shaking, yet

LAST NIGHT

Last night she expired
She was retired
Spirit had transpired
threw her in the fire

Last night she had a final dream
ate blueberries with whip cream
so serene
feeling like a queen

Last night she had her last fight
Last juicy bite
She's no more uptight
Now she'll take her flight

she strokes his hair, "Hi sweetie." "Hi Mom," he replies in a somber tone. "I made

MONEY DOESN'T MATTER

Money doesn't matter anymore
once lives are gone
when family is dead
and they are burned into ashes
watching their body buried underground
as the crane drop dirt over their coffin creates a suffocating
feeling
when realizing their soul is gone
only a carcass is left
A lifeless body in the coffin with makeup, her favorite dress, and
Barbie doll
With gems filling your room, but you are alone
Money doesn't matter anymore

your favorite breakfast this morning, a Spanish omelet with extra cheese," says

mother as she pulls back the kitchen chair from the table to sit her precious son

Keep On Moving

down. The young boy notices his mother's black eyes are puffy on her pale and fragile

PLANS CRUMBLE

Sadly
plans crumble
like soft sand castles
under violent waves
nothing is as it seems
the lovers relationship is as fake as dreams

skin as she sits down to eat with him. This morning she is disheveled, but she acts as if

THE DEATH OF THE CAT

Feeling socially retarded without my kitty
so pretty
watching her breath become deeper and deeper
walking
slower
sloooooower
sleeping
longer
looooonger

nothing happened last night…as if her son would have never known about her violent

CLEO AND ME

Our friendship was based on slapstick jokes,
A very simple way, we could relate.
This is how we became a friend of rogues,
Even though our minds come from a different state.
If wild mood swings would come my way,
I would voice my opinion and start to complain.
She would just ignore it and walk away,
I glared at her knowing it would not be the same,
the very next week - when I saw her,
We tried to go back to our sinister ways,
But I realized, there was no depth and no cure,
This was not a relationship going through a phase.
       It did hurt me, perturb me, I knew it had to end,
       This girl had to grow up for me to be her friend.

quarrel. She continues, "I have to work late today, so I'm going to leave your dinner

LET GO

Let go
Let the freedom flow
Let go
Make room to grow

Find your own way
Don't follow
Find your own way
Don't wallow

Let the situation
sticky operation
of sorrow
drift on

Smooth operator
sly perpetrator
let it go

Savor the moment
look deeply into his endless loving eyes
cry in his arms
and say goodnight

in the fridge," mother serves him, and lovingly looks at him with her dark glossy eyes,

NOT UNTIL THE SUN GOES DOWN

I'm not going to sleep until the sun goes down
You can get a big dinero
PORQUA?
FOR A PAPEL
that can change your life
make it right
I think you need to take me out to dinner
I'm hungry
Don't hesitate
I'm not going to sleep until the sun goes down
Lo Siento
what's your palabra?
Put on a happy face
You were just going to disappear like that
Chico or chica
goodbye hombre
te amo

"remember I love you." *After school, the boy plays basketball with his friend, and he*

SIZZLE FIZZLE

If it
fizzles

make it sizzle

going to die, so it's worth a try
live like it's your last day

make the memories
dreams come true

make life worth living and fighting for,
explore

Throw your shyness out of the window
How badly do you want it?
How hard are you willing to work for what you want?

forgets about the violent night. "Hey, do you want to come over to my house?," the

SOLACE IN YOUR MIND

Find solace in your mind
Find peace no where else
Moving, improving, removing, approving and disapproving,
Still restless in your mind

savor in the sun
on lover's beach

Keep on moving
keep on grooving

Short lived romance
what was his plans

Gray Days
putting my tears away for her
Gonna face the grey day for him

We know your leaving soon but we need you now
the time is now

boy's friend asks, "I have this new game at my house that we can play." The boy

SHY GIRL

Talking to her is like conversing with a fly,
she doesn't listen and is difficult to capture

avoiding the limelight
hoping to escape from the dimly lit room,
continuously bumping the screen window,

until caught by your large
mammoth hands
clasped together

you shake your closed hands
to feel the power of life you have now possessed
feeling the vibration of the fly,
strong little thing almost squeezing out of my hand
the little wings are so delicate
you gently squeeze it's little self
squishy then release

now that you have caught
you put it up to your ear
buzz-buzz-buzz

Silence

It has nothing to say
after all that work

It has nothing to say
feeling empty
where has the vibrant energy gone

It wants to escape
desperately peaking it's head out of your hands

you walk to the backyard and set her free
never to see her again

thinks about it then says, "I can't come." The boy begins to walk home with

It's like conversing with a fly,
she doesn't listen and so shy
difficult to capture
but once invited into her rapture
you can see her fire burn
seeing her soul shriek and churn
hoping to escape from the iridescently lit ballroom,
where asses are grabbed and male packages shot,
The smell of perfume, women that plot,
for the bride and the groom tie the knot

his head down regretting he turned his friend's offer down because the boy comes

EVENING SONG

Full moon rising on the waters of his heart,
He holds his lips apart.

Promises of slumber leaving shore to charm the moon,
Rest while twilight-keeps,
He sleeps,
She'll be sleeping soon.

He curled like the sleepy waters where the moon-waves start,
Resplendently gleams,
He dreams,
Lips pressed against her heart.

home and finds that he is alone in an empty house with a note on the refrigerator by

UNLOCK HOPE

The moon holds the key that unlocks the portal of deception
everything that is whimsical

float around and feel fat
bloated with chocolate and cream
the dream of the syrup spilling out of the mouth

The sun locks in for 12 hours straight
no where to go but face ahead
chest sticking out
a serious tone
claustrophobic
It's like eating Styrofoam

mom. *"Hi Sweetie, Sorry but I'm going to be coming home late tonight so I left you*

THE PERFECT LIFE

As I read your palm today
I saw trouble, but I didn't tell you
I know where you are going and what you see
What you feel
The reading is turbulent
You are not aware of your karmic journey
Mental traveler
The life, the life
I can feel your fear

dinner in the fridge. I love you and kisses." He grabs the note and throws it away

WHERE THE TRUTH LIES

Free your subconscious where the truth lies
Spreads it's legs
Get out of your head
Let your impulses drive you
Because that is the real you
Forget being polite
Be real
Free from the chain of society

then he grabs his dinner and eats his chicken in front of the television until he

TONIGHT

Tonight is his destiny
Tonight is his flight
It's tonight he strikes
streets full of fright
when he destroys
He finds pure joy

Stay inside
please save your pride

It's not you he wants
it a man who's gaunt
he likes to flaunt
who he wants to taunt

he's an oppressor
transgressor
aggressor
money stealer
unfair dealer
squealer
feeler

At night he strikes
hurts more than a dog bite
tough boy on the street full of fright

eventually falls asleep on the couch as father is nowhere to be found. After midnight

SERPENT

You're like a slippery serpent in the trees,
out to hurt, destroy, and heckle me
with your charm,
smile and joyous glee
you lie and taunt
and take want you need
and then you flee
so shiny with glee
and moist
cold and moist and so shiny
your fake charm

You just use me
trick me
To eat from the poison tree

mother comes home and picks him up and puts him in bed. The next morning at the

FEEL THE DANGER

Exploding lights
dynamite
knives in flight
thrown in with spite
tension in the air
strikes the affair
Feel the danger
           Feel the stranger in the room

Where did you go,
where did you go

tension
tightens your arms
flexing to disarm
Alarm rings
accusations fly
you try to deny
Feel the danger
           Feel the stranger in the room

eruption
burst of flames
sweaty hands
who to blame
terrible thoughts
my stomach in knots

breakfast table the weary mother kisses her son, smiles, and gives him a hug, "Have a

stomach in knots
terrible thoughts
acid reflux
paranoia
it's my phobia

someone is going down
hit the ground
nerve showing through my skin
shaking, heart palpitating
negative vigor
men dressed in suits
with his hand on the trigger
as the innocent dance
We must leave
I warn you
angels screaming
in my ear
to disappear

good day and go get 'em today. I'm going to be working late tonight, so I will leave

VENGEANCE

He has taken her for granted
So she has disappeared
lost in the vast city of weirdo's and crazy men shouting in the street
Pushing through the city of slimy personalities
searching for the gold, jewel and treasures

Time is her friend
learning to use it to your advantage
learning how to manipulate time
destroying her enemy with time
It may take one month, 2 years, 10 decades
But will use time as her friend

time will kill her enemies softly
during time of patience
long awaiting hours
when she had to wait until the big day
waiting with practice
until this grandiose day arrives
work hard during the in between time and she will have a splendid life
she struggles between the super ego and the underbelly

you your dinner in the refrigerator." "Again?," the boy asks. "I'm sorry sugar, yes, again," mother sighs. "Where is dad?," the boy inquires. "Well...He's on a business trip and I'm not sure when he is going to be back," mother gently tells him as she

The Sun Peaks Out

sighs, "I have to get going...I love you." At school, he forgets about his night as his

YOU ARE SO FABULOUS EXTRAORDINARY, EVEN GORGEOUS WHEN YOU SMILE AND LICK YOUR LIPS AND TOUCH MY THIGH WHEN WE WERE IN CANNES AND LOOKING SO FINE EATING GUMMY BEARS OF RED, BLUE, AND GREEN SINKING INTO YOUR PEARLY TEETH AND DOWN YOUR DEEP THROAT AND HANDSOME JAW LINE, THAT MAKES ME WILD BY THE WAY, WHO KNEW YOU WOULD LOOK SO GOOD WITH WHIP CREAM ALL OVER YOUR UPPER LIP; DANCING WITH YOU IN THE FAMILY ROOM WAS SO EXONERATING AND BLISSFUL THAT I WANT TO RUB YOUR BELLY AND TICKLE YOU WITH A PHEASANT FEATHER; AND BRING IN BELLY DANCERS TO SURROUND US WITH A SYNERGY OF LUNACY.

Oh My!

friend offers him a new question, "At my house we have a huge screen T.V. you have

MY STARLET

You opened up my heart and soul
you are my special one
I tried so hard to get close to you
but you didn't know
you are my starlet
who is a million miles away

got to come over." The boy looks at him, "Ok, I will go home with you, but I have

THE GUEST

invited guest
gets undressed
they lay at rest
as he stroked her hair
and kissed her breast
feel the zest

uninvited guest makes him depressed
she's a jest
after a request
to leave
she realized the messed
up situation
so she left

to come home first then we can meet." The boy runs home after school to his desolate

SHE'LL NEVER FIND

She'll never find
Never find
Never find
Never find
Find love

It's the same situation
Only with a different guy
Shy, shy, shy

Before it starts
it's already gone
Cry, cry, cry

If you could just take back your words
She might forgive you
Sigh, sigh, sigh

They'll have to agree to disagree
be free
bye, bye, bye

It's a hopeless love
messed up situation
why, why, why

She's still mad
and hopes you
die, die, die

She just dreams of tomorrow
on her bed and
lie, lie, lie

house and sees his mother's letter on the fridge. The boy throws it away and writes a

MISTAKE

He's waiting for her to leave
She's his newest pet peeve
avoiding her every step
sitting in the next room
She can feel his tender heart in the
next room
suffering
trying to keep cool

She can feel his spike
harpoon her heart

He smokes his pain away
ringlets dissolves
his anger
makes his pain
today is a special
smoking day
he stays away from her

letter back to his mother. "Mom, I'm going to Jimmy's house after school. I will see

LAST NIGHT

She saw you differently
Your body had banished
only the steam of your soul hung in the clear moonlight
A most exquisite soul
So genuine and clean
like a bright white smoke swirling
bigger and floating into the sky
eyes suddenly appear and flicker
within the night like two yellow bugs

you when you get home." Then the boy rushes over to Jimmy's warm home where

TWEAK PLEASE

What a bright light
burst through a shivering darkness
bodies blend and disappear
breathless eager
gleaming in your arms
reborn
in the thick translucent night
living forever in an instant

his radiant mother greets the boys with cookies, and after a fine dinner of pork chop

A MILLION DIRECTIONS

There are a million directions
But you are not one
So many avenues
different attitudes
Choose one

But you are not mine
Even with desperate time
I am undone
Frustration begun

A million directions
Too many objections
Reflections
Affections
Deep Connections
Rhythm sections
Many erections
Picturesque collections
Sweet inflections
Tasty confections
exquisite selections
handsome projections
You are perfection
But you are not mine

A Million Directions

and mash potatoes, Jimmy's father puts on a kung fu movie for the two boys. "It'

WHEN THE LIGHT TURNS OUT

When the light turns out
your color disappears
the face fades away
Age, height, color, flaws
don't matter
it's just you and your lover
just pure bliss
feeling every crevasse of his body
learning about his birth mark on his ass
becoming intimate
exploring the unseen
and untouched
finding the eroticism that drives him wild
and ticklish spots
it's those nights that
make experiences great

getting late shouldn't you call your mother or father and tell them you're here,"

SWIRLING EMOTIONS

unexplained my feelings
swirling in the air
being with you
silently, the unexplainable
becomes understood
Sometimes words cannot
fix the world
but understanding can

Jimmy's mother asks. "I wrote her a letter, but my mother works late," the boy

ONLY YOU

Wanting to open a life with you
only you sharing a soul with you

taking a deep breath
there you are
Picture perfect
reaching out to catch you
but you disappear
where did you go

Please
don't leave me
you are gone

COMMUNICATE

In order to relate
we need to communicate
if we communicate
we can set a date
so we can relate
no one will win the debate
challenge our fate
I just can't wait
be out real late
procreate

on a business trip and I don't think he's coming back," the boy becomes sad.

GOSH DAMN

Gosh Damn –
been through the gammit
of men
and then
and now

Whine and cackle
as they pack all
of their emotion into one big
blow
and gust of wind
with particles striking the eye
it all goes black as she squints and rubs her face

Jimmy's mother gives him an empathic look and tells him, "Well, I'll call your

THE MURDERESS

The Murderess finds herself in the chapel looking for forgiveness
Not right in the head
Too many things got in our way
Too many problems
Too many decisions
Too many people
I had to be with you

I have not suffered enough

Forcing me to get rid of the problem
Pushing me to the limits
Off the edge
They were yelling at me
It was nonsense
They would not let me see you

And now that we are together
I don't know what to do with you

If we do not run now we will be separated forever
They will take me away from you
And I will not be able to live
I will perish

So I will come here to the chapel
In hopes to be granted forgiveness
My secret love
I've gone through hell for you
A blacken heart

Hedonistic ways allowed me to be with another
Cheating on you with another
Realizing that I wasted so much time on other garbage

mother and tell her you are here, and you can stay here as long as you want to." The

I realized that I have only one love and it's you

without you I have been so lonely
suffering alone
Anguished soul without you
So many have stopped me in my tracks
Taking me away from you
I was tricked
Duped in the worst way

But now I know better
So I took care of the problem

But now we must run and find ourselves a new home
Together where we can live

boy looks at her and finds comfort in her tender eyes. They smile and he sleeps

HE'S HAD IT

She as fake as dreams
not as she seems
    It's not safe here
    He has to disappear
    from her dirty plot
sick of all her lies
that keeping him up all night
Dressed in black and white
concealing her wicked ways

soundly as the world gives him relief and comfort from all the pain. ~After one coitus

EMOTIONALLY SLUTTY

She let it all hang out the first time they met
And now regret
to reveal so much
to touch
upon her hearts content
that was pent
up with anger and love
from above

night the young girl sneaks back in her house through the backdoor and hides into

MISTREATED LOVERS

We've been bad to each other
Mistreated emotions
Miscommunication
Misunderstanding
Flaking on each other
Purposely missing each other
Timid with each other
Always thinking about each other
but never calling each other

her bed. Under her soft warm covers she smiles and thinks about the fun she has just

OBSESSED

Why do you find yourself obsessed with the untouchable?

The unbelievable
Unconceivable

Those as tough as a statue

Why do you like to torture yourself believing you have a chance
At their love
What do they have that you don't

Why do they charm you in a way that makes your heart hurt and linger for more pain

The heart feels heavy
As you indulge in their beauty

Staring at them is too painful and gives you sleepless nights

All you can do is stare
pretend that they love you back

had…she was in love. The next day, morning sickness interrupts her sleep, and the

CREATURE OF RANDOMNESS

Creature of randomness
Not of habit
Insanity each night
With whom shall he fight
Verbal abuse
Drug related excuse
Drinking at the bar
Ladies from afar

Randomness strikes
Unexpected car crash
With unexpected bikes
The two men smash
Flash
  Flash
      Flash
While the other steals his cash
And walks away

young girl finds herself in the bathroom feeling dizzy as she is in disbelief. She looks in the mirror and rubs her belly and becomes worried. From the drug store, the young girl franticly buys a pregnancy test then rushes back home and finds out in her

Racing Thoughts

bathroom that she has tested positive. The young girl cries in her room as if the grim

On a full moon words make love
when the moon is empty they fuck
sometimes soul kissing gently
other times raunchy necking
elusive
no excuses

                          The night is my friend
                          I cloaks me like royalty
                          I feel safe in its creepy arms
                              Mysterious mood

                          The words are beautifully chained together
                          like a necklace kissing the nap of your neck

reaper himself showed his face because how is she going to tell mother? On the

Have you ever sat down to listen to her?
                                        Don't feel bad no one has...
                She's there, in the corner like a little spider
        empty and alone

                        One

As I was meditating, I see Mr. Spider
I asked Mr. Spider
why do you spin your web
what is your purpose
he explains, " My Dear, it is my table cloth"

phone, the nervous young girl calls her boyfriend, "Come over, I need to talk to you."

Even after the caveman's fire has burnt
the smoke ascends
the twist and turns
contorts itself
into many intimate shapes images
that can only be imagined

  thought
It captures the essence of the future
it tells stories
it's the other
sending us a message
the spirits talk to us this way

                                                The wild expressive voice
                                                    lies deep within the gut
                                                   and subconscious mind
                                                       a place of fear and hope
                                                         temerity and brilliance

What day do you think you are going to die
I think it's going to be a Monday
because I hate Monday's
it's going to be during the winter solstice
so I'll celebrate my death day instead

"What for?," he says alarmed. "I want to see you," the young girl tries to seduce him

For $29.95 you can own the anti-depression pill
    And if you act now we will throw in Tear Of Joy
  Absolutely free

           Words like drawstrings untied verbs
              through the hurtful language
          sweet seduction relieves the pain
          a single black pen seals the blame
                    kiss your sorrow
                healed by tomorrow

I am but the wind caressing your neck
the howl kissing your ears
the blinding sun warming your face
if you wish to kiss my words
feeling faint as you speak
then I'll come closer to kiss your cheek

    I'm a writer and a fighter in a picturesque world
      that refuses to read the lines married to verbs
          that translate the inundated words
        that delineate the scenes of the slaughter
       and let the carnage linger in your mind

over the phone. "Do you miss me?," he flirts back. "Yes, oh yes, I miss you," she

                              looking like a corpse
                                       like death itself
                              what has become of him
                                         very scraggly
                        Can he be saved or is it too late

Quiet, I want to hear the vibrations of the marble statue

Late at night

alone in the room, through the corner of his eye

a movement

looking up

there is NOTHING

MIND IS RATTLED

ALL AROUND is normality

or is it

SWEARING IT WAS THERE DAMN IT

answers back. The young girl anxiously waits for him to show up at their favorite spot

The lunar eclipse made us wild,
each of us went our separate ways

to fulfill our destiny,

oddly enough it was

                              Agreed to disagree
                                he's still a bitch
                           he needs to understand
                                 He cannot switch
                                     he's wrong
                                   he so wrong

                              What are your principals

                               what are your motives

                               what are your morals

what are your gifts

what do you stand for

what do you detest

what do you enamor

where the tree hangs low. "Hey baby," he sneaks up behind the young girl and hugs

Mind is else where
           feeling disconnected
from people nature
                        air
        the planet - time-
don't understand
            miss understood

She saw the Angel of Death
On her left shoulder
He followed her for a week
She provoked him with her substance abuse
And the Angel of Death warned her
She saw the Angel of Death

her then gives her a kiss. The young girl smiles and looks in his eyes, "we are going

Perfect world
he shouldn't have asked for a perfect world

he should have dreamed that life would be glamorous

dreaming is killing him

wake up

this reality is killing him

Which god shall we chose

the skinny guy on the cross or the plump happy man

shall we give up bacon

find the chakras

just stay away from the bone crusher

to have a baby. "What?," he lets go of her, and the young girl is silent and waits for

gossip

she chops it up like freshly smoked steak straight from the grill and uses a cleaver to tear it up and quickly delivers it to the family

they devour it and want more   she chops her up and spits her out to others   she gets the fire going and leaves no innocent person behind

feeling like another statistic

Another accident

Another fucked up victim

A mistake

Made randomly

I like the music that turns people's heads

shocks them, rocks them and makes them dread

his reaction. She shakes with nerves and is breathing heavy. "Are you sure?,"

We are all fallen Angels
brought on Earth
to fend for ourselves

She was never "that" girl
the one you could adore
She was never "that" girl
that girl next door

Boy A: You're not going to manipulate me!

Girl B: Manipulate is such a harsh word.
I like to call it broadening your horizons.

upset. *"Yes, I took a pregnancy test,"* she tells him. *"Well, maybe it's wrong you*

I can't help it
I'm no good at being human

                         He loves to magically dance with his words
                              He loves to arch and raise his arms
                                        close his eyes
                                  letting his ears follow

Overtone
your life is already preplanned
you are born with limits
physical and emotional limits
likes and hates
personality
what do you do
is a result of your destiny

have to take it again," he is furious, "Go home and take it again." He looks at

The dance of the words the dance of the tongue
elaborate way of answering a question

                              do you think when we are dead
                                    we will see our faults
                                 and see all who we hurt?

Distance of a man and a fortifying plan
that already existed
some day they'll see our different way
of love and forgiving play

I have never been able to keep up with the rest of the world
I have always had to create my own pace

her. "Go now," he repeats and then he walks away. The young girl's heart starts

I escaped one reality ------> to get trapped in another
The transition is so

heavy on my heart

what can I do?

```
I sit here while my emotions grab me at the neck
It grabs my shirt and drags me into a rage of
fire that I cannot control
```

```
Born out of the womb and work your way down
to the grave
```
these are the only two certainties we know

  and all the time alone

racing as she suddenly becomes anxious, feeling scared and alone, so she rushes home. Months later, the young girl's stomach becomes bigger and bigger, and her mother looks at her funny. "Are you pregnant?," her mother demands with an upset tone. The young girl is silent. "Are you pregnant?," mother repeats. "Yes," the girl

whispers and begins to cry. "It's that fucking boy's isn't it?," mother yells. Mother is

furious. "Yes," the young girl answers. "What does he think?," mother interrogates,

but the young girl is silent. "So, your adult enough to have sex but your not adult

enough to answer me," mother throws words of anger at the girls face. The young girl

answers slowly, "I'm not sure...I don't think he wants it." Mother slams her hands on

the table and walks away leaving the young girl embarrassed and says, "we are going

to have to go to the doctors to get a check up." Nine months later the young girl has

the baby. She holds her baby and smiles for she has found her real love and

a beginning of a new life.

So, what are you waiting for start writing?

AND In the beginning...

www.ingramcontent.com/pod-product-compliance
Lightning Source LLC
Chambersburg PA
CBHW031645040426
42453CB00006B/219